CAPRICORN
December 22–January 19

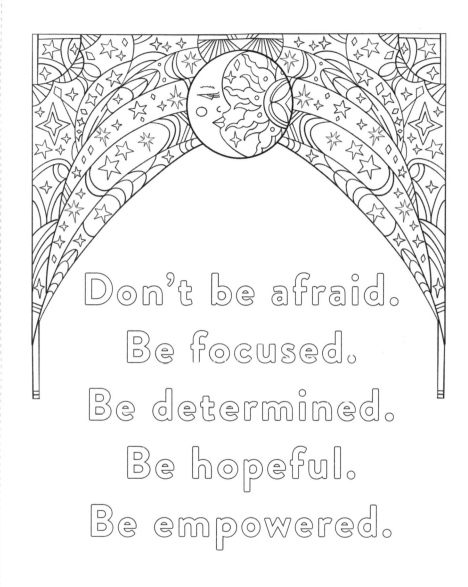

Don't be afraid.
Be focused.
Be determined.
Be hopeful.
Be empowered.

✧ Michelle Obama ✧

PANSY

winter

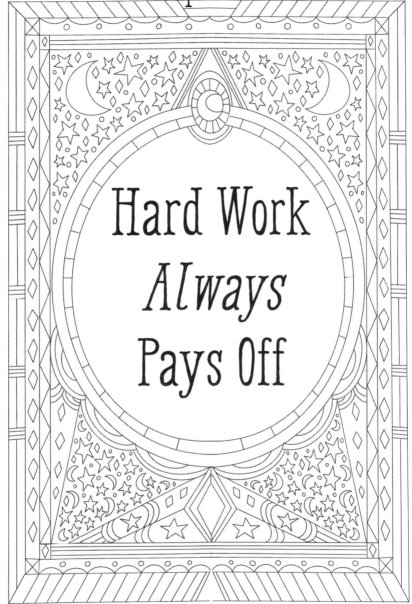

Hard Work *Always* Pays Off

Confident
Tenacious
CLEVER
AMBITIOUS
FOCUSED

RULING HOUSE

10

The House of Recognition

CAPRICORN

✧

I welcome the opportunity for change

✦ ✧ ✦

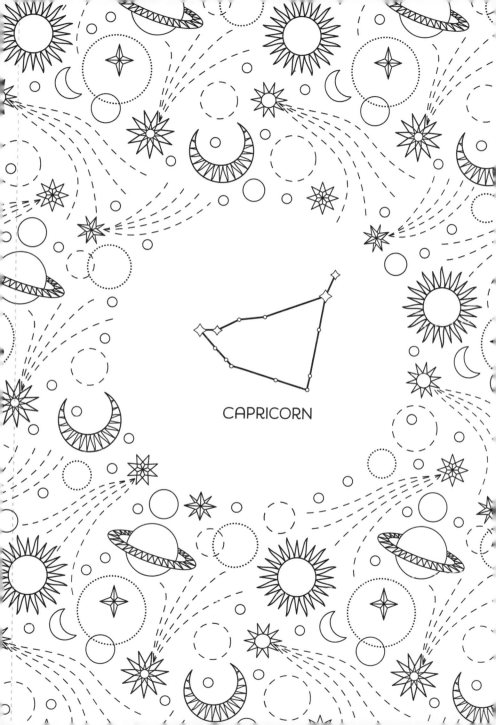

CAPRICORN

Aries

Taurus

Gemini

Cancer

Leo

Virgo

Libra

Scorpio

Sagittarius

Capricorn

Aquarius

Pisces

Earth Signs

Taurus

Virgo

Capricorn